Write a Money Making Business Plan

JUMPSTART YOUR BUSINESS PLAN, USING A TEMPLATE BASED ON A REAL STARTUP. COMPLETE YOUR BUSINESS PLAN IN JUST A FEW DAYS

Bill Yarberry, CPA

Table of Contents

"I was afraid to go out on my own, but my former boss gave me a jump start by telling me the most encouraging two words in my life. One day he came into my office and said, 'You're fired.'"

- Anonymous

Introduction

Entrepreneurs need a starting point with their business plan. You can easily find books which identify virtually every possible business topic, cram them into shotgun shells, and then blast away. However, you may be at stage one, working to get your business off the ground. If so simple, intuitive guidance is probably what you are looking for. Research shows that having too many choices paralyzes many people—they prefer to start simple and build incrementally[1]. To keep your business plan doable within a few days, I've pared the template (see https://bit.ly/2GHOy9s) down to only essential elements. The template, heavily altered ("obfuscated") to protect identities of all parties, is a snapshot of a real telecom services business, just as it launched. Although some details are not relevant to your venture, the book gives a real life perspective of what is needed: a presentation of the vision, how and when you will reach milestones, pros and cons of approaches you have considered, team members, and the recipe for your "magic sauce"—what makes your company stand out from others.

Without denigrating my own book, I think of it as "good enough" rather than a paragon of business plan excellence. Here's why: for human decision makers there is a strong—very strong—bias towards confirming what they already think. Suppose you buy a Fiat 124 Spider and later that week see one parked at a prestigious restaurant, along with other high end sports cars. Most people would note with some satisfaction, that other successful people bought a Fiat Spider. The majority would not think "I see so many other cool sports cars here. Did I make the right choice?" The second thought is unlikely due to a common human failing— "confirmation bias." Once you have decided, particularly when that decision is associated with time and money, your brain automatically sets up filters to tell you how smart your decision was and simultaneously diminishes all contrary input. You

---

[1]

https://www.researchgate.net/profile/Benjamin_Schneider9/publication/299214015_Understanding_customer_delight_and_outrage/links/5704332f08aef745f7148e87.pdf. Accessed on 2-11-2019.

have unconsciously and inadvertently reduced the odds of successfully using new information to improve your actions or decisions.

What does this have to do with a business plan and why should that plan only be "good enough?" Answer: if you put *too much effort* into developing a perfect, polished, and professional-looking plan, you risk confirmation bias[2]. You could become so invested in the correctness of the plan that you ignore the subtle warning signals of customers, the marketplace or even your own employees. This is all subconscious. Entrepreneurs, as a group, are bright. None of them would consciously cross arms and say "I'm closed to new information because otherwise I'll have to change my beautiful business plan."

A few years ago, a manufacturer of high end yachts ran its financials in search of changes which could improve profitability. After further research, the company developed a strategy of selling a lower cost line of yachts which, of course did not project the same level of luxury and quality as their original line. They believed that the volume plan would increase total profits. About halfway through the implementation of the new strategy, a flaw in the business plan became clear to everyone. The plan ignored the psychological effect on workers of the transition. Long-term employees were accustomed to a culture that celebrated top craftmanship and personal pride in the product. Even the slightest flaw got immediate attention. With the new plan came routine, assembly line production. A mundane product line, even with six sigma quality control, was not the same. You can probably guess what happened next. The workers could not adjust their mindsets overnight. Years of luxury oriented work gave them a confirmation bias against anything mass produced. The fact that the middle market was not sensitive to the extreme luxury touch did not matter. The company spent unexpected millions on the transition.

My advice is to take the basic business plan here, modify it for your business, do all the standard document quality processes (spell check, editor or outside person to

---

[2] "Confirmation bias, also called confirmatory bias or myside bias, is the tendency to search for, interpret, favor, and recall information in a way that confirms one's preexisting beliefs or hypotheses. It is a type of cognitive bias and a systematic error of inductive reasoning. People display this bias when they gather or remember information selectively, or when they interpret it in a biased way. The effect is stronger for emotionally charged issues and for deeply entrenched beliefs." https://en.wikipedia.org/wiki/Confirmation_bias. Accessed 2/18/19.

review, an accountant to verify the numbers), and then start using it. "Good enough" means reasonable quality and strategic thinking but not so much effort that it creates serious confirmation bias. Your "baby" could be ugly or perhaps only her outfit is ugly. Just be ready to listen to both positive and negative feedback and change the plan to meet reality head-on.

This business plan is a snapshot of a startup with the time pressures, changes in direction, changes in the market, and other unknowns that will undoubtedly show up in your business. It's easy to change, as it should be.

I have included a copy of the business plan in Word format at the following link https://bit.ly/2GHOy9s. Feel free to download this document and change in any way that you like.

Early in my career I won a bid from the Institute of Internal Auditors to develop an application auditing course. I teamed with a group of IT auditors to develop the course. We delivered by the deadline and the Institute seemed happy with work product. Later I found out, through informal sources, that the course materials had been substantially changed. I asked someone at the IIA why they had outsourced the development of the course if they intended all along to change it. Their response: they never intended for the course materials submitted to be a final or even close to a final version, regardless of what it looked like. What they wanted was a place to start. It's much easier to start with something on paper than it is to load 500 sheets of blank paper in your printer and start writing. I hope you view this business plan in the same light. Take this and change it to suit your needs and business sector. At the end of the book, I list a few example topics that the business plan does not cover. Look at these and use them if they apply to your business; there are many others.

I wish you success.

Bill Yarberry, CPA
Houston, Texas USA
February 14, 2019

Good Enough Business Plan

Caveat: All names, organizations, dollar amounts and other references to either businesses or individuals in this mockup business plan are fictitious. Conceptually, the plan is based on an actual startup, but all details have been intentionally obscured.

T-MOREREVV Corporation
Contact: Alex Perry, Jr. ap@t-morerevv.com 713.555.9811

The Mission: To develop a financial alert, monitoring and optimization system that helps clients reduce their telecommunications expenses.

The Market: According to Business News of New Jersey, the average Fortune 500 company saves $10K per month from a professional telecom review. The total market in cost savings is in the hundreds of millions, possibly billions. Our potential customers include two groups: (a) organizations that use more than $200K annually in telecom services and (b) consulting firms that already have a cost management/business efficiency practice; these firms could use our package/training to offer telecom cost management services to their clients.

The Product/Service: T-MOREREVV has two revenue sources: (a) traditional, contingency based cost savings projects and (b) a product for the ongoing reduction of client telecom expenses ("Telecom Kost Kutter, TKK")
The core idea behind TKK is the recognition that organizations no longer have the time and staff to recognize and resolve billing errors or opportunities for proactive cost management. TKK uses tariff databases, current and historical customer billing information, peer firm data and numerous experience driven rules to identify and summarize telecom expenses, errors and alternative, more cost effective

approaches. Web based and parameter driven, it provides condensed, "need to know only" cost information.

The Business Model: T-MOREREVV will continue to perform contingency based cost management reviews as a means of a) generating operating cash b) gathering information about customer needs/preferences and c) developing relationships for future product sales. The major focus of the firm is towards product development. When complete, the TKK product will provide income via a) lease and maintenance fees for the system b) upfront product training and c) custom installation.

The Technology: The TKK product's value lies in its logic, use of peer data and consolidation of exceptions/recommendations into an extremely condensed format. The technology is strictly an "off the shelf," web and traditional database architecture.

The Competition: There are approximately 500, mostly boutique, firms in the US that specialize in telecom cost management. The majority of these consulting groups are small and only semi-automated. Typically, these firms are contingency based (i.e., charge a percentage of the savings found). Larger firms such as VelocityTel, Stonehouse, MinTel24 and TexasTelMin offer many services including: "A to Z" telemanagement (outsourcing), routine billing analysis and other more complex services. These firms often require a substantial customer commitment and ask the customer to relinquish control over some or all the telecom life cycle processes.

T-MOREREVV Corporation Business Plan

Executive Summary

T-MOREREVV Corporation intends to capitalize on the following trends:

- Increasing total telecommunications expenditures.
- Expansion of telecom infrastructure.
- Continued error prone billing by providers.
- Inadequate human bandwidth in most organizations; lack of time to identify errors and possible efficiencies.
- Need for a product that proactively manages telecom expenditures using an analytical engine to identify exceptions and significant variances from peer firms.

Earnings will come from the following sources:

- Audits of telecom expenditures, contingency based. We perform a detailed review of an organization's telecom expenses and earn a percentage of the savings. We are in this business now and are earning revenues. Occasionally, clients may look for hourly or project based telecom consulting.
- Licenses for a yet to be developed product, Telecom Kost Kutter (TKK). This product will generate a recurring fee from both consultants and end users of telecommunications products (i.e., all organizations except the carriers). It takes input from multiple sources and provides timely, condensed cost relevant information based on a powerful analytical engine. Although call accounting products have existed for years, TKK will go well beyond these mature products to provide unique "financial alerts" based on statistical models and experience based logic; it will also provide unique comparative reporting, showing customers how their costs compare to peer groups.
- Consulting, training, certification and front end implementation of the TKK product mentioned above. Consultants need this training so they can be experts for their clients and end users need the product to be properly implemented and tailored to their organization's infrastructure.

Our customers will include:

- Consultants
- Organizations with more than $100K in annual telecom expenses.

Rather than focusing exclusively on product development, with the associated risk of many months without revenue, we will continually perform telecom cost savings audits. As a result, we will gain both steady revenue and an increasing base of telecom billing knowledge. We will also refine the product by identifying areas of strong customer interest.

Initially we will use a combination of manual and semi-automated processes to perform the audits. As we develop the Telecom Kost Kutter product, services can be scaled to include many more firms. Proceeds from TKK are expected to outstrip audit revenue by early 2019, providing more than 70% of total T-MOREREVV revenue by the end of 2020.

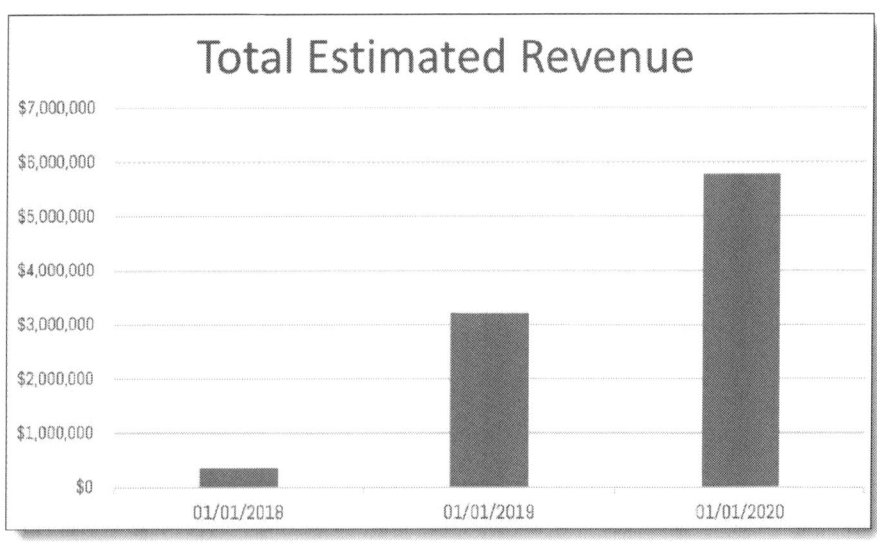

Figure 1. Total Estimated Revenue

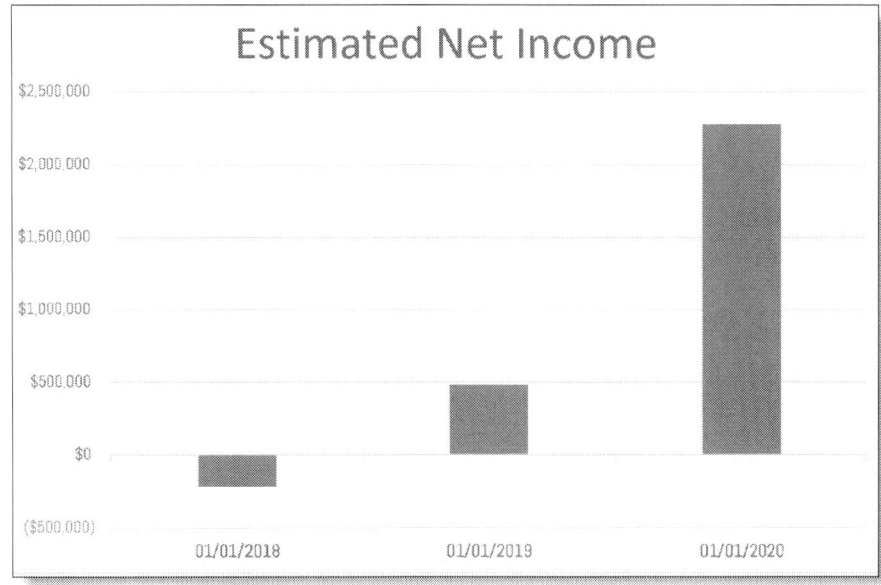

Figure 2. Estimated Net Income

Objectives

T-MOREREVV Corporation's strategic objectives are:

- To become the primary solution provider focusing on the analysis of telecom billing, with the objective of driving down telecom costs for enterprises.
- To provide the same solution to independent consultants with additional features and training, providing them with capabilities not readily available to their own clients.
- To provide in-depth training and ongoing support so that users of the TKK solution (both in-house corporate staff and consultants) can effectively use the system in their business environment.
- To become a nationally recognized telecom cost management provider by reducing the direct and indirect costs of our clients.

Mission

T-MOREREVV will develop a product that helps organizations reduce their telecom costs. In the same sense that Turbo Tax makes a vast store of tax expertise available to the general consumer, we intend to package telecom cost management knowledge in a simple to use software product that is periodically refreshed with carrier and peer company information.

We are squarely on the side of the enterprise and business consultants who provide cost management services to their clients. The product equips non-specialists with a plethora of analysis and monitoring tools that allow them to identify and implement cost savings within their organizations. It is also valuable for organizations with a large telecom infrastructure—while they could develop some reports and web interfaces themselves, this package obviates that need. It significantly reduces the time and effort required to obtain cost management information. A unique feature, the peer comparison analysis, is not available to most firms except through expensive consulting engagements such as those from World TEL-IQ.

The ability to continually provide telecom industry and pricing information is a key element of T-MOREREVV value to the customer. We will continually modify our services and products to provide higher value, ultimately becoming an industry recognized standard.

Company Summary

T-MOREREVV Corporation, formed in Houston, Texas, in August 2017 was founded by Alex Perry, Jr. and Alfonzo Geld. Their two previous firms, TMKR and East Texas Telecom Consulting LLC, respectively, merged to create a more powerful organization with more breadth and depth in areas such as SRM (sourcing relationship management), product development management, business development, project management, outsourcing, technical research, telecommunications auditing, marketing, and technical writing.

T-MOREREVV is committed to helping the consumers (business enterprises) of telecommunications services reduce their telecom costs. To accomplish this primary goal, we provide services—the telecom cost management review; and a product -- Telecom Kost Kutter2.

From a day-to-day perspective, T-MOREREVV is not overhead intensive. Since most of the value of the firm is in intellectual property only modest operating expenses are required for operations. We maintain a no-frills but efficient work environment where ongoing cost management projects can be managed and product specifications developed.

Company Ownership

T-MOREREVV Corporation is a "C" type corporation. The articles of incorporation were filed at the Office of Secretary of State in Austin, Texas on August 26, 2017. Our filing number is 44172458.

Ownership and management team are as follows:

- Alex Perry, Jr., President and CEO
- Alfonzo Geld, Corporate Secretary and CFO

Products and Services

Telecom Cost Savings Audits, Contingency Based

Contingency based telecom cost savings audits are well established. They are based on the reality that most organizations have inefficiencies and billing errors that they cannot realistically uncover without additional professional effort (time) and expertise. A few examples of cost savings:

- The lines that connect a firm to its local and long-distance carriers may be more than what is needed to carry the traffic. Some of those lines can be eliminated.
- Bills from the long-distance carrier could have a rate per minute that is considerably more than the contractual, agreed upon rate.
- The telecom architecture does not fit the current size and/or the business structure of the organization, resulting in higher long-distance charges than necessary.

T-MOREREW is performing these services now. For example, we audited a North African based quality inspection company, identifying $68,000 annual savings out of an annual budget of approximately $350,000. Our revenue is typically 50% of the savings.

Product, Telecom Kost Kutter

The Telecom Kost Kutter product has not yet been designed at the detail level or programmed, except for a limited prototype. This is our only product and is expected to generate most of the revenue for the firm after 2019. Following is a high level diagram of its inputs and outputs:

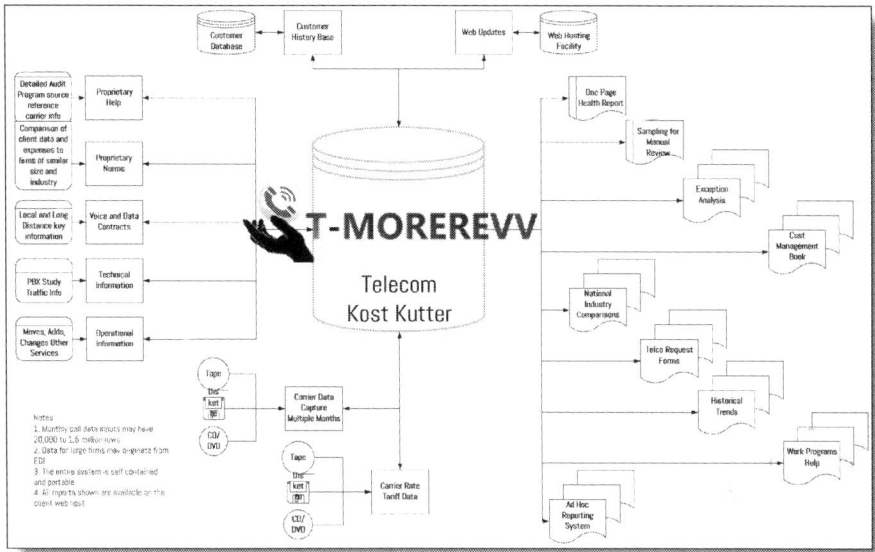

Figure 2.5. Conceptual diagram of core product, TKK

The core idea for the product is as follows: IT and telecom managers are increasingly busy with day-to-day projects. They do not have time for the analysis that needs to be done to minimize costs. Clerical or lower level personnel may have the time, but they are typically paid to process bills routinely, without the benefit of "what if" analyses and other tools. Hence the organization needs a tool that will do at least some analytical thinking.

Telecom Kost Kutter includes two key analysis capabilities: a) The red flag early warning application and b) peer comparison and trending module. The red flag application has an analytical engine behind it that looks at many factors, evaluates their urgency, and then reports only those that need management attention. A red flag summary could include two items or twenty. It could say "Five calls had durations over ten hours each", "Interstate long distance rates billed are approximately 30% higher than contract rates," and "Calls from the Atlanta office to the Denver office are sufficiently high that dedicated lines should be investigated." It is the telecom manager's "junk yard dog" that reduces the danger of financial surprises.

The peer comparison and trending analysis module provides more strategic information. It looks at more than twenty expense items, ranging from calling card setup fees to hourly rates for voice server maintenance, and graphically profiles the customer in relation to peers, based on size of telecommunications infrastructure. It also trends the customer's own history, allowing proactive management of resources, negotiations with vendors, etc.

Market Analysis Summary

Market Segmentation

Our target market for direct contingency services includes all firms, except telecom providers, with telecom expenses exceeding $100,000 per year. With expenses of $1,000,000 or more, the benefit/effort ratio increases significantly. Houston, Austin, Dallas, Ft. Worth, and San Antonio based firms are preferable due to lower out-of-pocket costs but even out of state projects can be completed, in part, from the Houston office.

Virtually all organizations (for-profits and non-profits) use telecom services such as local and long distance calling, calling cards, toll free services. Hence, we have the luxury of a market that includes nearly all organizations with annual telecom expenses greater than $100,000.

The market for sales of our Telecom Kost Kutter (TKK) product includes the following two classes of potential customers:

- Direct users of the product, having $100,000 or more in telecom expenses per year.
- Consulting firms ranging from boutique size to big four accounting firms. These firms would like to open a new channel of revenue by providing telecom cost cutting services to their clients. Our product will appeal to them since they cannot otherwise justify the skill ramp up and ongoing expense of maintaining expertise in the area.

Target Market Segment Strategy

Our target customers can be further stratified as follows:
Cost Savings Projects (audits) for Enterprises:

- With annual expenses of $100K - $1M, having limited telecom expertise in house and/or divided responsibilities. For example, some organizations will divide staffing between telecom and facilities management.

- With $1M to $ 5M annual expenditure ranges who have a larger telecom staff but are understaffed (due to general workload or specific projects).
- With more than $ 5M annual expenditures who appreciate the value of an independent perspective. These customers will often be fully aware of the opportunities for cost savings and will direct the work towards specific regions, types of expenditures (e.g., local versus long distance) or vendors.
- With a history of problems arising from telecom billing and overcharges. Sometimes specific events, such as a facility move or merger, may drive the need for a focused review of expenses.

Telecom Kost Kutter for Enterprises

TKK could be effective for firms with as little as $100K in annual telecom expenses. However, we realistically expect that only enterprises with annual telecom expenditures greater than $250K will have an interest in the product. Below that level, the sales effort is not worth the revenue obtained. As shown in figure 3, we anticipate the largest enterprise revenue to come from organizations with $5-$10M in annual expenses.

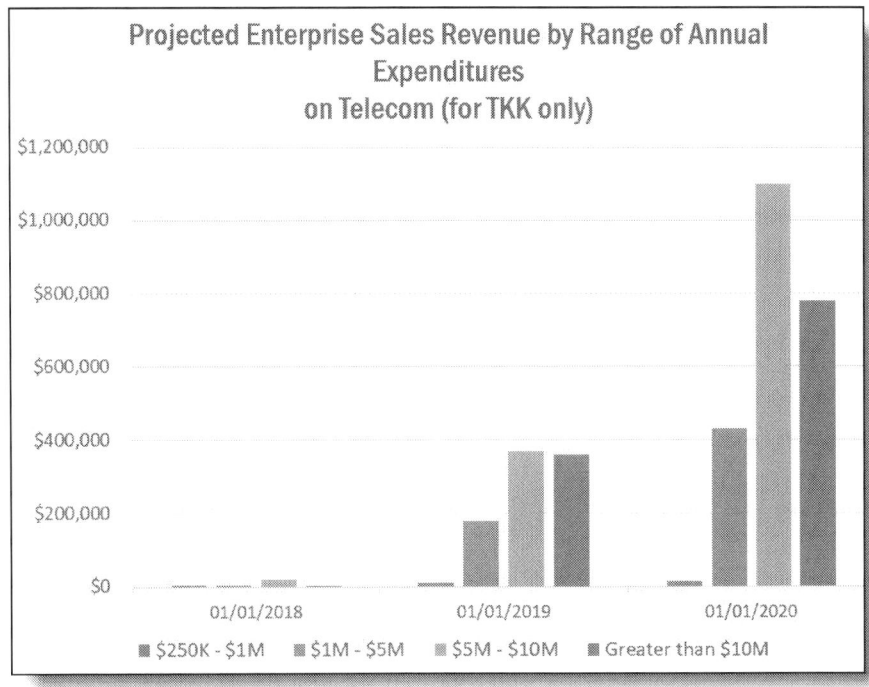

Figure 3. T-MOREREVV Revenue projection based on size of client telecom spend

Telecom Kost Kutter for Consultants:

Sales to consultants will show a different trend — maximum revenues are obtained from the largest consulting firms, such as a large regional firm. Teaming of telecom cost management with consultants such as CPAs has precedent. For example, Comogistics in Houston has a relationship with CFC Florman for consulting services in telecom.

Figure 4 shows anticipated revenues by size of consulting firm.

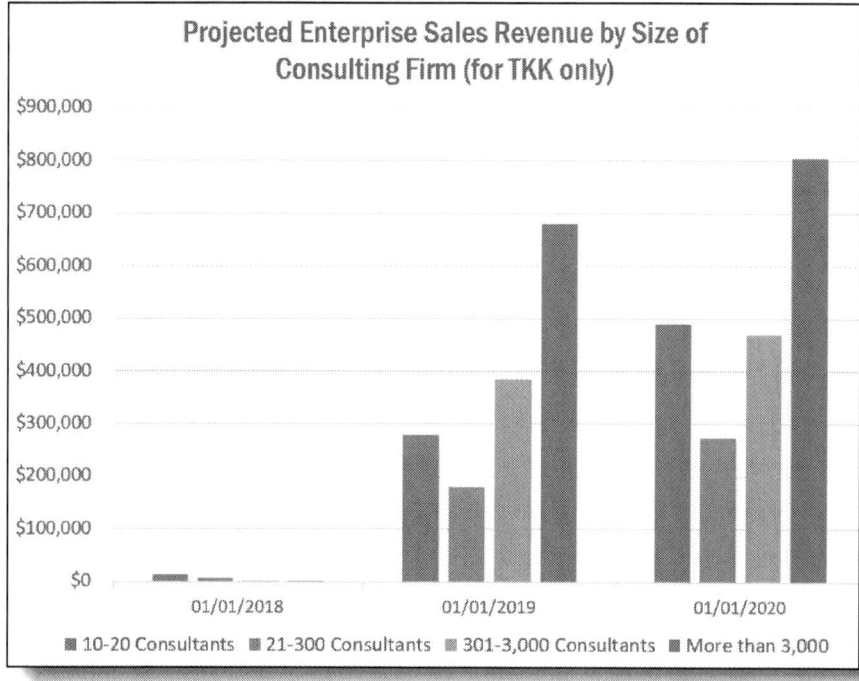

Figure 4. Project Sales Revenue by Size of Consulting Firm

Service Business Analysis

Contingency based telecom auditing firms are typically boutiques. Often started by ex-carrier individuals, they vary widely in quality and scope of services. They are usually limited by geography since the contingent model means that out-of-pocket expenses would be at risk for out of town assignments.

Even though there are many firms in this service space, our anecdotal experience is that only about a fourth of the firms that could benefit from a review have had one. Part of this opportunity is due to the nature of boutique consulting, which relies heavily on networking and personal contacts. Most of the boutiques cannot afford to advertise. Also, they are limited in manpower, since audits can sometimes take months to complete. Telecom managers sometimes resist cost reviews, fearing that they will appear "asleep at the wheel" in front of superiors.

We target higher level executives to obtain sales and then deal with the telecom manager only on an operational level. Another factor that enhances our ability to market is our level of automation. Most telecom auditing firms use limited automation and are therefore human resource constrained (cannot scale).

Competition and Buying Patterns

VelocityTel and Intercellar2 are examples of firms that are selling telecom cost reduction products. Intercellar2, created in Australia by Pomodoro Consulting, has not been selling well, according to internal sources. VelocityTel has spent considerable venture capital in business development (over $100M so far). However, their model of "one stop shopping" for least cost telecom services has not been successful and it requires a long sales cycle.

The following are example competitors in the telecom cost management business. Voice Reports estimates there are approximately 500 firms that specialize in cost management for telecom and electric utilities.

- CurrTel Lab: Offers "n-control" expense management system. According to their website, their product provides the ability to "electronically download billing data directly, run processing routines, post expenses to General Ledger and present management reports over the Internet all without human intervention."
- MaisonHouse: Offers the following services a) "integrated, modular Xtantres suite of applications enables you to automate internal ordering processes, reduce billing errors, and centralize the processing and tracking of your communications assets b) Our Professional Services team provides the installation, integration, training and consulting expertise you need to realize results faster e) Or, if it makes more sense for your business, you can outsource your communications management via our Managed Service."
- Tellima Neo-affinis: Offers financial management (outsourcing), cost containment, historical auditing, competitive analysis, RFP/FRQ management, bill checker program and general professional services.

- Telantheric Associates: A) Analysis and review of existing services, including a comprehensive bill audit. This program is designed to optimize services while reducing telecom costs. B) Assistance in RFP development, tariff comparison initiation, negotiation on client's behalf or proposal review to determine pitfalls or areas where additional negotiation is required. C) Continuing administration to handle projects, including but not limited to adds, moves, changes, monitoring measurements, bill management and payment, and telecom planning. D) nationwide seminars on auditing techniques."

Because contingency work for the same firm usually occurs on an 18, 24 or even 36 month basis, it takes several years for a firm to develop a reputation in a geographic area. For example, Jeffry Falmer and Associates, a boutique in Houston, has been in business for nearly 15 years and obtains all customers by word of mouth and reputation. The larger firms have advertising budgets but then have the financial pressure to rush the jobs, potentially alienating clients (cream skimming). Another competitor in Houston, Telekinesos, focuses on getting clients into better contracts (i.e., changing carriers). Although Telekinesos claims to audit for 127 separate cost savings elements, the net result is often simply a carrier change. Hence, that firm is essentially a reseller with a thin patina of cost savings covering their services.

Another player, Secundigravida in Plano, Texas, offers a voice server firewall that includes some cost savings features. However, there is only a 15-20% overlap in functionality between the two products. Also, we intend to discuss mutual referrals with this group as Telecom Kost Kutter gets closer to implementation.
Most potential clients haven't given this service much thought, so education and ability to get to the right person in the organization are prime success factors.

The Telecom Kost Kutter product has breadth of functionality and yet is available to mid-tier firms. The offering is thus unique in the industry.

Differentiation from competing products (such as call accounting systems) is provided by two key features:

- Financial Alert Module. Using an analytical engine and feeds from multiple data sources, the financial alert module identifies those exceptions and opportunities that should be brought to the attention of the telecom organization. Only exceptions that warrant review are highlighted. Competitors may have exception reports, but they do not combine them into a single system that provides a condensed analysis. Today, finding cost savings opportunities requires sorting through many reports and time consuming review. Our system requires no more than a few minutes per month of management attention.

- Peer comparison module. Using survey and client data, we provide telecom cost data for firms of similar size and usage patterns. Many firms have paid outside consultants tens of thousands of dollars merely to assure themselves that a negotiated offering is competitive. This module obviates that need. Also, even the best agreements tend to become uncompetitive towards the end of the contract. By noting any relative slippage over time (going the wrong way on the normal distribution curve of pricing), the telecom group can pressure their carriers to preemptively adjust pricing to be more competitive.

Strategy and Implementation Summary

Competitive Edge

The following attributes separates T-MOREREVV from others in the telecom cost management space:

- Founders have a rare combination of audit, telecom management, IT, business development, accounting, product development, and sales. CEO has a strong background in product development management, business development, strategic planning, and sales. CFO is a CPA with years of audit and telecom experience.
- Plans include simultaneous product development and execution of ongoing telecom audits.
- Bottom up, low overhead approach used. Founders will do much of the initial product specification work.
- Publication of telecom books and articles provides T-MOREREVV with visibility in the marketplace.
- Empathy for and perspective of telecom management keeps product focused on solving practical, day-to-day problems of telecom cost control.

Marketing Strategy

We do not intend to use expensive advertising. We will market as follows:

- As we perform audits, we will use our own product. This will enable the customer to see it working in the most visible and customized way possible. It is likely that any customer large enough will be interested.
- We can use associations, such as the IIA (Institute of Internal Auditors) to reach mid and top tier consulting firms. For example, one of our competitors, Cymograph - with a much less comprehensive package - was nearing a deal with Gaston Garfield Group days before that firm disintegrated.
- Partnerships with non-competing telecom groups, such as Secundai, can help spread the word.

Sales Strategy

t-MOREREVV's sales strategy is based on referrals, publications, and eventually limited advertising. The sales cycle for cost management is a long one, particularly for the larger corporations. Typically, the cycle goes as follows:

- Make initial contact through personal contacts, networking or advertising from previous clients.
- Present the concept in an informal setting to a decision maker or near decision maker.
- Present formally to financially oriented individuals, the CIO and others with a cost perspective. The telecom manager may resist, fearing negative findings. Submit the draft contract for client review.
- Answer questions and resolve issues offline. If essential, provide a free half-day cursory review of potential savings (a diagnostic).
- Attempt to schedule work as soon as possible. Do not start work until a contract is signed.
- Proceed with contract.

The client may not fully understand the contingency model; there may be concerns about a windfall. The details of T-MOREREVV compensation need to be thoroughly explained and expectations should be set early on. For larger clients, the contract will be strongly worded to ensure we can collect any large sums identified. The "unjust enrichment" perception must be resolved by using the " dry hole" analogy for oil well drilling—the successful ones pay for the dry holes.

We will use a standard sales force automation product to maintain customer records, follow-up to-dos, etc. Initially Alex Perry, Jr.   will be responsible for all sales efforts but we expect to use additional resources by the end of 2019.

Sales Forecast

The tables at the end of this section show estimated sales for product and audit services. While the audit revenue is relatively predictable, the revenue from leasing product could vary considerably, depending on market acceptance.

Additional revenues include:

- Consulting contract with Bit-Wise Computing Analysis including retainer fee, and commission.
- Miscellaneous consulting fees including various forms of consulting such as the chargeback analysis project for Bit-Wise, consulting fees from Pyrausta Nubilalis (an existing client brought into the business by Alfonzo Geld) and other voice/networking consulting projects.

Primary sales derive from contingency based audits until the Telecom Kost Kutter product is ready for the market.

Contingency audits yield revenues proportional to the telecom spend of the firm reviewed. For example, assume a firm has $1.5 in annual telecom expenses. If we find 3% savings (very conservative number), then our fees will be $1.5M x 3% x 50% = $22,500. At a 7% savings (average), fees are $52,500, and at 12% it will total $90,000.

We are aware, from private conversations, that one of our competitors, Co-operative Synergistic communications, has identified $500,000 in savings on long distance alone, in one year. These savings were accomplished with one person doing sales and project management along with another individual doing spreadsheet analysis. Co-operative Synergistic communications, per their web page, charges 50% fees. Assuming a 5% findings rate, Synergistic was able to process $10M in long distance alone (does not include local and other types of telecom savings).

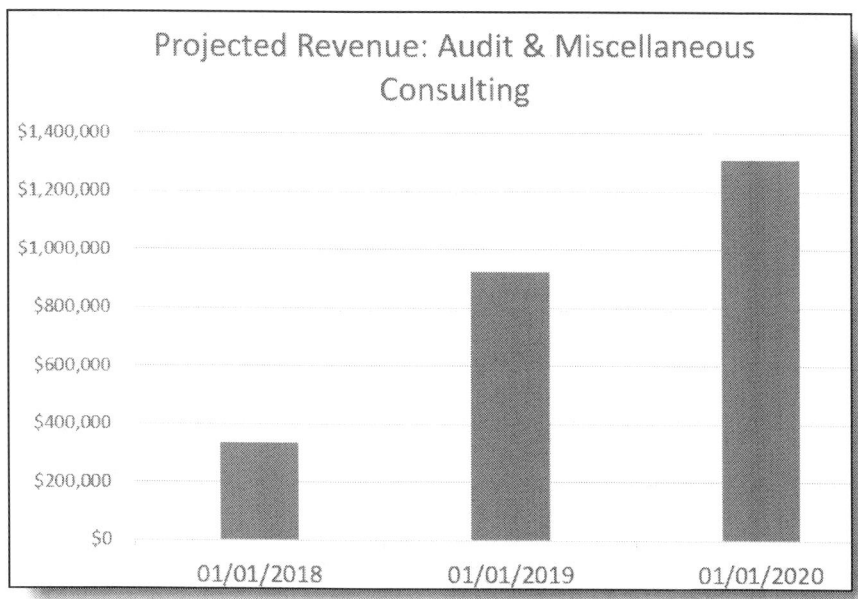
Figure 5. Projected revenue from audit and consulting

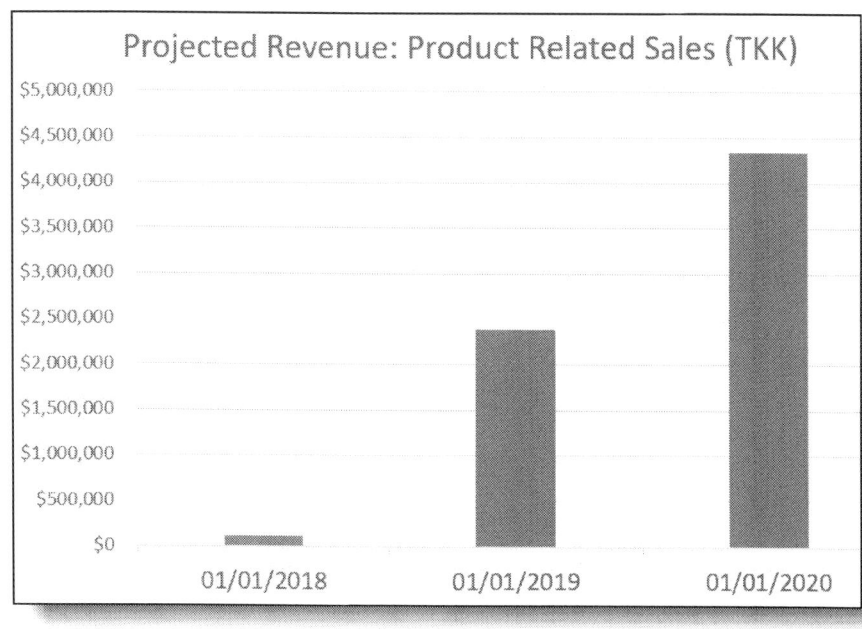
Figure 6. Projected revenues from product (TKK) related sales

Milestones for First Year

Date	Activity
August 2018	T-MOREREVV incorporated as a Texas C corporation
October 2018	Completed successful audit of Aristides Greco SA. Revenue approximately $15,000. Identified $38,000 in savings for client.
November 2018	Completed website, internal methodologies for more efficient reviews. Reached tentative agreement with Annubus Hotel (Galleria area, Houston, TX) for a January review. Held first meeting of T-MOREREVV solutions advisory group at Zerrni Hotel.
December 2018	Completed Phase I of a cost management review for Mustus Corporation based in Hilfe, Wisconsin. Revenue of $6,000. Developed specifications for eight utility programs to increase the efficiency of audits. Two programs completed. Tentative agreement with Yearbye Group, Inc. for a review in January, 2010.
December 2018	Complete preliminary specifications for core product (Telecom Kost Kutter)
Projections	
January 2019	Complete version 2 of standard cost management procedures manual
February 2019	Complete negotiations with appropriate telecom database provider for monthly feeds to Telecom Kost Kutter.
March 2019	Complete feed specifications for at least four major IXC's and two LECs
May 2019	Complete first working version of Telecom Kost Kutter product
June 2019	Identify at least one beta site for product installation Product ready for market; at least one sale anticipated.

Management Summary

T he founders of T-MOREREVV, Alex Perry, Jr., Alfonzo Geld and Virginia S. Puntank, are long time professionals in IT and Telecommunications. Alex's background is in outsourcing, management consulting, product development management, strategic planning, business development, and sales. Alfonzo's hands-on experience in managing telecom projects, both at Ensconce and Pricket Enterprises, provides the ability to immediately generate revenue from ongoing operations.

Virginia S. Puntank, with long project management experience with BLHIT Corp, provides technical support and contract administration support.

Short bios:

Alex Perry, Jr. is responsible for developing and implementing T-MOREREVV's overall strategic direction and developing and managing client relationships. Prior to T-MOREREVV, Alex served as general manager of a business process integration systems and services company serving the energy industry.

Alex has over 25 years' experience in the information technology services industry holding a variety of consulting and management positions in business operations, sales and marketing. He has international experience having spent five years of his career living and working in the Middle East and Asia.

Alfonzo Geld, CFO and cofounder of T-MOREREVV, brings both private accounting (Sr. Manager, Prichet Corp) and large scale telecom management experience to drive down operating costs for clients. He has over twenty-four years of experience in telecommunications cost management, IT application development, internal audit management, and outsourcing administration.

Prior to joining Prichet Corp, Alfonzo was Director of Telephony Services for Ensconce Corp. He was responsible for the operations, planning, and architectural design for voice servers and related voice communications systems supporting over 8,200 employees.

His other experience includes the valuation and sale of microwave towers and licenses, GHAT contract negotiations, and PBX RFP development. As time permits, everyone except Alex will participate in the projects, particularly early on, when cash flow is so critical.

Others may be brought on board on a spot basis if additional help is needed. However, they will not be part of the core team in 2019, nor will they be drawing salaries. Alex and Alfonzo, as CEO and CFO respectively, constitute the board of directors.

All three members of the current team are deeply experienced, with a full complement of skills coming into the job. No training (other than ongoing personal education) will be required.

To obtain insightful business advice as well as higher level industry contacts, T-MOREREVV has added the following senior level board of advisors:

Yeatsian Meror - General Manager, Aristides Greco SA. Since joining Aristides Greco 20 years ago, Mr. Meror has held various technical and management positions. He was instrumental in the formation of ARISTIDES GRECO Certification in the United States and then assumed the position of Regional Manager for GRECO's Western Europe. Mr. Meror returns to the US, from the Netherlands, to take up the position of General Manager for Aristides Greco certification activities in the Americas, with responsibilities for North America, Mexico, Central and South America. He holds an MS degree in Engineering from Oxford, an Executive MBA from Plato's Academy and a BA degree in classical Hittite from Texas A&M University.

Dr. Arida Schipperke - Principal and Director of the Data/Risk Analysis Practice at ThrallFord, Inc. Dr. Arida Schipperke is Principal and Director of the Data/Risk Analysis Practice at Exponent, Inc. He is a former faculty member at the Langlerly School of the University of Cumquatington, where he directed research and taught economic and statistical analysis of business, government, and nonprofits organizations. Dr. Schipperke has a diverse consulting portfolio in globalization of business, corporate governance, executive compensation, and corporate performance management. In these engagements he has applied managerial economics and operations research methods to improve the deployment of human resources, supply chains, market competition, health care, and government services. Before joining Exponent, Inc., Dr. Schipperke was a Principal Consultant at Cuthbert Gladstone Associates, Inc. He holds a Ph.D. from Superfluous Logarhea University, a Masters in Nanotechnology from Yuffa Technical Institute at Buffalo, and a Bachelor of Environmental Plethorics from Texas A&M University.

Personnel Plan

The personnel plan reflects the need for ongoing management (CEO and CFO), an analyst as the work grows, and a marketing/packaging professional. The marketing professional is not fundamentally a sales position; instead, it is someone who can take the prototype TKK (Telecom Kost Kutter) and build the marketing infrastructure around it—documentation, press releases, training, customer usability, etc.

Due to the wide availability of part-time telecom experienced individuals, staffing of the audits can be ratcheted up incrementally. At the point where ongoing volume is assured, permanent analyst positions can be created.

By the end of 2022, we anticipate the following full time staff:

- CEO, Alex Perry, Jr.
- CFO, Alfonzo Geld
- Director of program management (Virginia S. Puntank)
- Director of Marketing (TBD)
- Analyst #1 (audits + data analyst)
- Analyst #2 (audits/product/training)
- Analyst #3 (audits/product/training)
- Analyst #4 (audits/product/training)
- Sales (Alex Perry, Jr.)
- Sales professional (2nd Q 04)
- Sales professional (2nd Q 04)
- VP of RandD (TBD)
- Developer #1
- Developer #2

Anticipated salary expense is shown in figure 7.

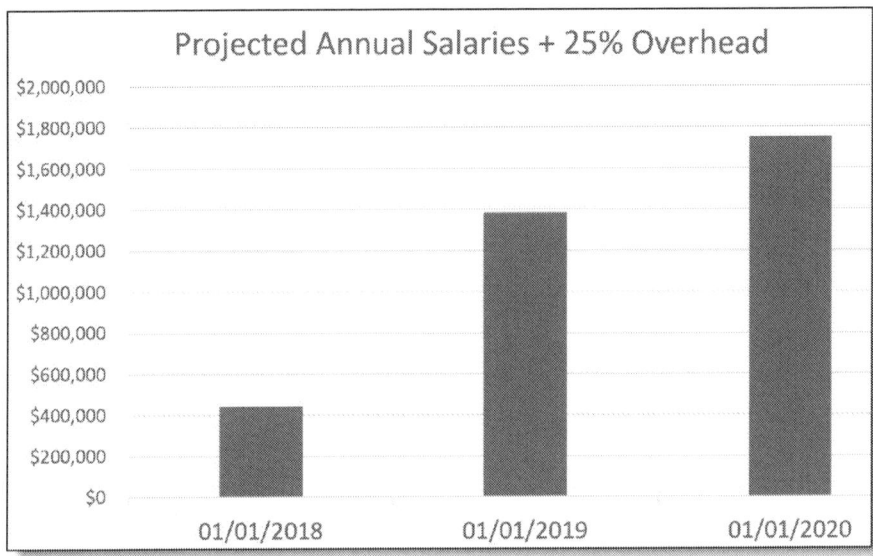

Figure 7. Projected salaries plus 25% for estimated overhead

Financial Plan

For T-MOREREVV Corporation, there are two scenarios that will affect success over the next three years:

- T-MOREREVV gets no external funding (equity or debt) and creates all value from internally generated funds. This will substantially delay the rollout of the Telecom Kost Kutter product. It will also delay the introduction of the Kost Kutter into our own audits, thus reducing the efficiency gains expected. Finally, one to two years may be required to fund web infrastructure equipment to roll out Telecom Kost Kutter in volume.
- T-MOREREVV obtains funding and is able to develop the Telecom Kost Kutter relatively quickly (within 4-6 months). This approach allows more of a focus on the product and its format, marketing strategies and technical infrastructure (web server, etc.). It shortens the time required to begin receiving revenue from sales.

We plan to pursue option #2. In early 2019, we will seek equity funding of $250,000. The proceeds will be used exclusively for product development.

Important Assumptions

Our financial plan starts with the assumption that the market for telecom cost management is substantial. According to a USA Yesterday report:

- The cost of telecommunications now ranks in the top five expenses for most companies.
- US business will spend around $403 billion in 2019.
- The Telecommunications Industry Association predicts that in 2021 the market will approach $600 billion.

While the unit costs for services such as long distance voice calls may be going down (eventually to become a flat rate), the number of services is going up so the total amount spent seems to monotonically increase. Also, the carriers continue to under fund their billing departments, resulting in routinely incorrect billing. The opportunities for recoveries are greater than ever. Rand Associates, a consulting firm, says that there are billing mistakes on phone bills 80% of the time.

Our plan is not particularly sensitive to small changes in overall US growth. Two factors seem to come into play: 1) if the economy is sluggish, the incentive to cut costs increases; indeed, it is politically astute for managers at all levels to be cost conscious and 2) if the economy is robust, there is more freedom for risk taking and therefore the sales cycle is not as long.

Projected Profit and Loss

Since we intend to expense all software development in the year incurred and there are no major non-cash expenses (e.g., depreciation) or revenues, the cash flow statement will show roughly the anticipated profit and loss. The cash contributed by investors should, of course, be subtracted from the ending cash flow to provide an approximate measure of profitability.

At the end of 2019, the projected cash balance is $2.8 million. Assuming an equity investment of $250K, the life to date profit of T-MOREREVV is projected to be roughly $2.5 million. By 2020, T-MOREREVV will be adding more than $200K per month to available cash. These projections are conservative.

Projected Cash Flow

Table 1 shows estimated cash flow for the years 2018 through 2021. In practice cash flow is presented on a monthly timeframe but has been shown by year to conserve space.

We are and will continue to be both a services and product company. By staying in the field performing contingency-based, cost reduction audits with real financial outcomes, we can ensure our product is relevant and practical for our customers.

T-MOREREVV Corporation
Estimated Cash Flow

Summary by Year

Sources:		2018		2019	2020	2021
Revenue from Audits	$	20,000	$	245,000	$ 1,214,496	$ 1,620,504
Revenue from software lease/training/consulting	$	-	$	114,198	$ 2,388,000	$ 4,333,500
SBA ("Mowdoc") Loan	$	-	$	-	$ -	$ -
Contribution from Investors	$	-			$ -	$ -
Misc Consulting	$	3,500	$	3,000	$ 3,000	$ 3,000
Analog Specs retainer	$	6,000	$	24,000	$ 24,000	$ 24,000
Analog Specs additional revenue	$	10,000	$	60,000	$ 60,000	$ 50,000
Year		2018		2019	2020	2021
Sales	$	39,500	$	446,198	$ 3,689,496	$ 6,031,004

Uses:						
Payment for outside developers	$	-	$	240,000	$ -	$ -
	$	-	$	-	$ -	$ -
Salaries (fully burdened)	$	-	$	-	$ -	$ -
- Alex Perry, Jr.	$	7,500	$	96,000	$ 166,500	$ 203,000
- Alfonzo Geld	$	18,000	$	102,000	$ 134,500	$ 158,000
- Marketing person	$	-	$	62,000	$ 107,500	$ 123,000
- Analyst (audits + database maint)	$	-	$	21,000	$ 90,000	$ 103,500
- Other	$	-	$	8,000	$ 102,000	$ 116,000

	2018	2019	2020	2021
Contractor Payments	$ -	$ -	$ -	$ -
- Adam C. Comptraner	$ 3,500	$ 30,000	$ 48,000	$ 48,000
- Others, as needed	$ 1,000	$ 12,000	$ 13,500	$ 18,000
	$ -	$ -	$ -	$ -
SBA debt service (7 yr note @ 7%)	$ 4,778	$ 19,114	$ 19,114	$ 19,114
	$ -	$ -	$ -	$ -
Overhead expenses	$ -	$ -	$ -	$ -
- Rent, Alfonzo Geld	$ 500	$ 3,000	$ -	$ -
- Rent, 3-4 person office	$ -	$ -	$ 10,800	$ 10,800
- Corporate telephone	$ 200	$ 1,600	$ 1,250	$ 1,200
- Transportation	$ 300	$ 2,600	$ 1,900	$ 1,800
- Meals and entertainment	$ 300	$ 2,200	$ 1,850	$ 1,800
- Computers, etc.	$ -	$ 1,650	$ 1,800	$ 2,400
- Office supplies, postage, etc.	$ 200	$ 2,000	$ 1,300	$ 1,200
- Internet connection	$ 200	$ 1,200	$ 1,200	$ 1,200
	$ -	$ -	$ -	
Expenses	$ 36,478	$ 604,364	$ 701,214	$ 809,014
Year	*2018*	*2019*	*2020*	*2021*
Estimated Net Profit	$ 3,022	$ (158,166)	$ 2,988,282	$ 5,221,990

Table 1. Typical projected cash flow statement.

Additional Topics to Consider

The business plan presented here is a scaffold. As technology, regulation, and the general business environment change, you should add to and revise your plan. Following are some potential strategies/trends to add:

- Lean startup constraints—how to minimize costs for everything non-strategic, leaving funds for your core business
- Social media
- Funding methods, including crowd funding (e.g., kickstarter.com)
- Analytics, machine learning, infographics
- Risk assessment (what could go wrong)
- Legal concerns, if any
- Supply, distribution and globalization
- SWOT: Strengths/Weaknesses/Opportunities/Threats
- Manufacturing, supply, inventory, quality control
- Break-even analysis
- Ratio analysis
- Elevator speech
- Order fulfillment and customer service
- Exit plan

Conclusion

A good business plan is a repository of intended actions plus a discussion of challenges, the means to accomplish goals, and enterprise strategy. It could be as narrow as "we will create the lowest cost, safe, renewal energy based vehicle in the South American market." Or as broad as "we will enable the fastest possible transportation systems for regions not previously served." Aside from applying for loans or communicating with investors, the best business plans engage your mind and imagination to consider opportunities, risks, and the timetable for action. Update your business plan frequently. Make it accurate, thoughtful, and creative but avoid the "irrevocable decision" mindset as much as possible. You may find your Excel spreadsheet and charting skills improving as you quickly revise schedules and intended actions. If so, great. On the other hand, if you find yourself hiring graphic artists to create the Mona Lisa of fixed[3] plans, not so much. I hope this short template helps you set up your business plan quickly, so you can get down to what matters—providing needed products and services to your customers and enjoying the financial rewards of running your own business.

Thank you for purchasing this book. I would love to hear from you. Contact me at byarberry@iccmconsulting.net. Negative, neutral, and positive comments are all equally welcome. You will receive a response to any emails within 48 hours. One more thing—all writers live and die by reader reviews on Amazon. If you like the book, I would greatly appreciate a review on Amazon. Just go to this book on Amazon and click on "write a customer review."

Best wishes,

Bill Yarberry, CPA
Houston, Texas
February 14, 2019

---

[3] The French even have a name for it, "idée fixe." Like the supposedly impregnable Maginot line in World War II, beliefs cast in unmovable concrete are often counterproductive.

About the author

Bill Yarberry, CPA, is President, ICCM Consulting LLC, based in Houston, Texas. His practice is focused on data analytics, IT governance, regulatory compliance, security consulting, project management and business communications. He was previously a senior manager with PricewaterhouseCoopers, responsible for telecom and network services in the Southwest region. Yarberry has more than 30 years' experience in a variety of IT-related services, including application development, data analytics, internal audit management, outsourcing administration, and Sarbanes-Oxley consulting.

His books include The Effective CIO (co-authored), What Top CIOs Know (co-authored), $250K Consulting, DPLYR, Computer Telephony Integration. 50,000 Random Numbers, GDPR: A Short Primer, and Telecommunications Cost Management. In addition, he has written over twenty professional articles on topics ranging from wireless security to change management. One of his articles, "Audit Rights in an Outsource Environment," received the Institute of Internal Auditors Outstanding Contributor Award.

Prior to joining PricewaterhouseCoopers, Yarberry was director of Telephony Services for Enron Corporation. He was responsible for operations, planning, and architectural design for voice communications servers and related systems for more than 7,000 employees. Yarberry graduated Phi Beta Kappa in Chemistry from the University of Tennessee and earned an MBA at the University of Memphis. He enjoys reading history, rowing, collecting antique fountain pens, hiking, and spending time with family.

His Amazon web page is www.amazon.com/author/billyarberry. Comments and questions are welcome. Contact email: byarberry@iccmconsulting.net.

Other books by Bill Yarberry

- ❖ $250K CONSULTING

- ❖ THE EFFECTIVE CIO

- ❖ WHAT TOP CIOS KNOW

- ❖ DPLYR

- ❖ GDPR: A SHORT PRIMER

- ❖ COMPUTER TELEPHONY INTEGRATION

- ❖ TELECOMMUNICATIONS COST MANAGEMENT

- ❖ 50,000 RANDOM NUMBERS

Acknowledgements

Samuel Johnson, the famous 18th century writer and creator of the first major English dictionary, said "He who is self-taught has a blockhead for a teacher." To some extent that applies to self-editing as well. I try not to do it. It is rare indeed to find people who can find all their own grammar faults. With that in mind, I give many thanks to **Carol Yarberry**, whose editing skill and acumen for discovering grammatical flaws never ceases to impress.

Permission and Disclaimer

In accordance with the U.S. Copyright Act of 1976, the scanning, uploading, and electronic sharing of any part of this book without the permission of the publisher constitute unlawful piracy and theft of the author's intellectual property. Thank you for your support of the author's rights.

While all attempts have been made to verify the information provided in this publication, the author does not assume any responsibility for errors, omissions, or contrary interpretations of the subject matter herein.

The views expressed are those of the authors alone and should not be taken as expert instruction or commands. The reader is responsible for his or her own actions and decisions.

Adherence to all applicable laws and regulations including international, federal, state, and local governing professional licensing, business practices, advertising, and all other aspects of doing business in the United States, Canada, or any other jurisdiction is the sole responsibility of the purchaser or reader.

The authors assume no responsibility or liability whatsoever on behalf of the purchaser or reader of these materials.

Printed in Poland
by Amazon Fulfillment
Poland Sp. z o.o., Wrocław